The Gospel, Sexual Abuse and the Church

A theological resource for the local church

**The Faith and Order Commission
of the Church of England**

The Faith and Order Commission began working on the area of theology and safeguarding in 2014, in response to a request from the lead bishop for safeguarding to the House of Bishops' Standing Committee for theological material that could complement what was being produced by the National Safeguarding Team in terms of policy and training. *The Gospel, Sexual Abuse and the Church* has been written by the Faith and Order Commission to meet that request. It has been approved for publication and commended for study by the House of Bishops.

William Nye
Secretary to the House of Bishops
June 2016

Church House Publishing
Church House
Great Smith Street
London SW1P 3AZ

ISBN 978 0 7151 1109 3 (Paperback)
　　　978 0 7151 1110 9 (CoreSource eBook)
　　　978 0 7151 1111 6 (Kindle eBook)

Published 2016 for the Faith and Order Commission
of the Church of England by Church House Publishing

Copyright © The Archbishops' Council 2016

All rights reserved. Other than copies for local, non-commercial use by dioceses or parishes in the Church of England, no part of this publication may be reproduced or stored or transmitted by any means or in any form, electronic or mechanical, including photocopying, recording, or any information storage and retrieval system, without written permission which should be sought from the Copyright Administrator, The Archbishops' Council (address above).
E-mail: copyright@churchofengland.org

Unless otherwise indicated, the Scripture quotations contained herein are from the New Revised Standard Version, © 1989, by the Division of Christian Education of the National Council of the Churches of Christ in the USA, and are used with permission. All rights reserved.

Typeset by ForDesign

Printed and bound in Great Britain by
Ashford Colour Press Ltd., Gosport, Hampshire

Contents

Preface by The Rt Revd Dr Christopher Cocksworth,   6
Chair of the Faith and Order Commission

How to Use this Document   10

Introduction   13

Section 1   18
We should strive to be a church where those who have been hurt by abuse find compassion, and people ready to travel patiently alongside them

Section 2   24
We should strive to be a church where those who commit abuse are called to face human justice, hear God's word of judgement and repent and believe the good news

Section 3   30
We should strive to be a church where all people are welcomed into open and secure communities that make known Christ's reconciling peace

Afterword   40
We need to be a repenting and learning church that recognizes past and present failures and the harm they have caused, and seeks forgiveness from those we have failed and from God

Resources for Further Study   43

Notes   46

Preface

In March 2014, the House of Bishops' Standing Committee, responding to a request from the lead bishop for safeguarding, asked the Faith and Order Commission of the Church of England to carry out some theological work on the subject of safeguarding. This request came in the context of a changing public landscape for safeguarding as well as a legacy of serious church failures in this area, most notably as recorded in the recent reports of Judge Sally Cahill and the Chichester Commissaries. It also follows on the public apology for the church's past failings on safeguarding at the July 2013 General Synod by the Archbishop of Canterbury.

Safeguarding children and vulnerable adults from the risks of abuse and responding well to abuse wherever and whenever it has happened are now high priorities for the Church of England, and rightly so. In recent years, the Church of England has re-launched its work on safeguarding at national level and has developed a national policy framework that includes a rigorous training programme extending to every level of the church, as well as appropriate forms of monitoring and inspection. This is in addition to the increasing work on safeguarding at diocesan and parish level. Changing the culture of the church so that safeguarding becomes fully embedded within it as an outworking of the gospel is a key objective.

In order for safeguarding work at all levels to enter fully into the life of the church, it is vital that every member of the Church of England is enabled to affirm the relationship between compliance with policy and faithfulness to the gospel – bishops, clergy and laity alike: good safeguarding is integral to the mission of the Church of England.

Preface

This is a theological task. That is not to say that it is a task reserved for the academically minded, although it will benefit from careful engagement with academic studies. It is a theological task because it concerns how we speak about the God of Jesus Christ in relation to the practical challenges the church faces here.

Safeguarding from abuse and responding well to it need to be grounded in the fundamental themes of Christian theology and thereby woven into the church's regular ministry of preaching and teaching. At the same time, safeguarding raises significant theological questions for Christians: questions about humanity, sin, grace, forgiveness, reconciliation and the church. Making space for grappling with the issues that arise here is essential if the church is going to be able to speak about God and about the gospel both when it is seeking to do safeguarding well and when it is reacting to situations where something has gone badly wrong.

Abuse happens in different contexts and can be of different kinds. The Faith and Order Commission intends to offer some reflection about that in another document, which will also consider in more depth the particular questions raised by Christian teaching about forgiveness and reconciliation in this context. Partly in order to keep the current text to a reasonable length, however, it was decided to concentrate on issues raised by sexual abuse, though we hope it will also be helpful for thinking theologically about all forms of abuse.

The particular theological 'lens' through which these issues are brought into focus in the document is ecclesiology – the doctrine of the church.

What kind of church are we called to be in order to face the challenges of safeguarding from abuse and responding well where it has happened? For Anglicans, dioceses, parishes and fresh expressions are all 'church', sharing unity not only in the national Church of England, but as part of the one, holy, catholic and apostolic church throughout the world. Our hope is that while keeping all those meanings of 'church' in mind, readers of this document will want to think in particular about the church community in which they are regularly involved, the church in the place where they are called to serve – their 'local' church.

Hence the subtitle of this publication from the Faith and Order Commission is important: *The Gospel, Sexual Abuse and the Church: A Theological Resource for the Local Church.* It is not intended to be a treatise for academic discussion, but a text to be used by Christian communities who want to think through how the church speaks about the gospel when facing the reality of sexual abuse, both in the communities it serves and as a crime carried out by its own members and officers. At the same time, it is not intended either to replace policy or guidance, but to be read alongside key documents from the diocese and the national church as a specifically theological resource.

First and foremost my hope would be that all who hold the bishop's license to preach and teach would read it carefully for themselves, along with all those who deliver safeguarding training in the Church of England.[1] I also hope, however, that they will find stimulating, challenging resources here to be used in their formal and informal teaching – training sessions, church groups, sermons, for example –

Preface

with clergy, laity, staff and volunteers. Some guidance on how to do that is given in the brief note on 'How to Use this Document'.

I am grateful to the members of the working group who produced the original draft of the text that follows. It has been through an extensive process of consultation, both formally with official church bodies, including the National Safeguarding Panel, and informally with particular individuals. It has been discussed and approved for release by the House of Bishops. I am particularly grateful to those who have participated in that process who are themselves the survivors of abuse. I pray that the document we have produced can make some small contribution to enable us to be:

- a repenting and learning church that recognizes past and present failures and the harm they have caused, and seeks forgiveness from those we have failed and from God

- a church where those who have been hurt by abuse find compassion, and people ready to travel patiently alongside them

- a church where those who commit abuse are called to face human justice, hear God's word of judgement and repent and believe the good news

- a church where all people are welcomed into open and secure communities that make known Christ's reconciling peace.

The Rt Revd Dr Christopher Cocksworth,
Chair of the Faith and Order Commission

How to Use this Document

This document is intended to be used as a resource for their work by those with responsibility for teaching and preaching in the Church of England, including clergy and licensed lay ministers, and those with specific responsibilities for safeguarding training. This dual readership is crucial. The intention is to help the whole church address the theological issues that inevitably and properly arise in a church context from reflection on the challenges of preventing abuse from taking place and responding well when it has happened. The goal is to support *both* those who are confident in teaching about scripture and Christian faith *and* those confident in delivering training about safeguarding in addressing such theological issues. The importance of strengthening the Church of England's capacity to do this is clearly indicated in the national Learning and Development Framework for safeguarding, and all those involved in implementing it should benefit from considering this document and identifying opportunities where it might be used.

One of the aims of the document is to help church communities do some theology together as they engage with necessary matters of safeguarding practice and training. Using it for teaching, whether in training sessions, sermons or the many other possible contexts, will however require careful adaptation of the text that follows. This is not a set of session outlines, or material that can simply be repeated verbatim in any context. It is, as the subtitle says, a resource. So, for instance, the framework of the three main sections could be used to structure a day event, or just one of them could be used as a focus for a single session, perhaps as part of a longer event where attention to theological reflection would sit alongside other training areas (as is implied in some of the module outlines within the national Learning and

How to Use this Document

Development Framework). As well as the main sections that seek to present theological thinking, there are discussion questions, suggestions for bible study and quotations for reflection. Again, these are likely to need to be adapted for each particular context, or their value may be in prompting others to come up with something more suitable and perhaps quite different.

It is crucial to ensure that all concerned understand that this material is designed to help people think theologically about issues that arise for churches in light of their commitment to following national safeguarding policies and practice guidance (which can be found at https://www.churchofengland.org/clergy-office-holders/safeguarding-children-vulnerable-adults/national-policy-practice-guidance.aspx) and diocesan procedures. These need to be understood as the essential background for any engagement with the document, including its discussion questions. The relationship between policy and theology is one that may be worth dwelling on in any teaching session. For instance, policy and practice guidance documents set out some crucial parameters for how the Church deals with survivors and also with individuals who may pose a risk, including known sex offenders, and these need to be understood and adhered to. This document complements these and offers an additional resource to help congregations respond to the moral and spiritual challenges potentially raised by safeguarding situations, such as how they think about the relevance of redemption, healing, judgement and repentance. That is theological work – but work that always needs to be undertaken with one eye on the policy guidance as well.

Ideally, teaching sessions drawing on this material might be co-led by at least one person with theological training and one person with safeguarding expertise. While that is not essential, if either area of knowledge is weak, care needs to be taken that people are directed towards appropriate follow-up and, if necessary, professional assistance. All who speak in a public context about abuse should be aware of the likelihood of people being present who have suffered abuse themselves and who may have particular needs for support during and after the event itself. Those who hold responsibility on such occasions will need to have thought through how they will respond to people wanting to speak about being survivors of abuse and ensure that information is offered at the beginning of sessions about how individuals can access support. If assistance is needed to advise on this please talk to the diocesan safeguarding adviser as part of planning a session.

Introduction

What kind of church should we be?

There is a gap between the kind of church we should strive to be and the church we see and are, in the face of the evil of abuse of all kinds. These failings require that we must first and foremost be:

- **a repenting and learning church that recognizes past and present failures and the harm they have caused, and seeks forgiveness from those we have failed and from God.**

This will be a recurring theme in what follows and the focus for the Afterword at the end of the document.

We should be:

- **a church where those who have been hurt by abuse find compassion, and people ready to travel patiently alongside them**

- **a church where those who commit abuse are called to face human justice, hear God's word of judgement and repent and believe the good news**

- **a church where all people are welcomed into open and secure communities that make known Christ's reconciling peace.**

The three main sections of the document that follow this Introduction explore each of these statements in turn.

What kind of church do we see?

- We see churches, including the Church of England, that continue to do a great deal of very valuable work with children and vulnerable adults, and have made significant progress in developing policies for safeguarding over the past three decades.[2] There are many examples of good practice in particular contexts. Yet we also recognize that this progress has taken a long time, longer than it should have done, and the price of delays has been high for those continuing to suffer from abuse. We know too that there is further work needed in achieving consistent standards across our churches in this area, and a consistent recognition that this matters to us urgently because the violation of a human being who is made in the image of God and for whom Christ died is intolerable.

- We see churches that are still fathoming the depths of past failures in keeping people safe from the harm of sexual abuse and in responding well to people who have been hurt by it.[3] While awareness and understanding of this subject have undoubtedly grown exponentially in recent years, Christian teaching has always held that this is very serious sin. Yet there have sadly been occasions when Christian pastors and leaders have not always treated it with due seriousness. In particular, there have been occasions when they have been more concerned with limiting damage to the church's public reputation – so closely bound up with the conduct of its clergy – than keeping children safe from harm, though they had no reason to doubt which was more precious in the eyes of God. That profound moral misjudgement has in turn shaped an inclination to manage abusers within the closed boundaries of the church's institutional life, rather than seeking to bring them to justice.

- We see churches that are beginning to engage with the vital and demanding task of listening carefully to survivors of abuse and learning from them and with them.[4] One dimension here is meetings by church leaders with individuals and groups. Another is seeking to make sure survivor participation is built into the continuing processes of policy development and monitoring. Alongside all of that goes a commitment to proper pastoral care that recognizes those who have experienced abuse in a church context in particular are likely to need a special kind of 'safe space' to begin to re-engage with the church at some level. Yet we know that we are at the early stages here, and it has taken us far too long to arrive.

What's different about the church?

Put bluntly, then, we see a church that is at last facing the reality that some of its members, including ordained ministers, have exploited their position of power to use vulnerable people for their own sexual gratification. Moreover, we see a church that accepts it has not always responded to cases of abuse with due care or responsibility, often failing to take full account of the trauma inflicted on victims, including the violation of what is sacred, and failing to appreciate the degree of denial and deception, including self-deception, of perpetrators.

In this regard the church is like some other institutions, and it will be investigated with other public institutions by the Goddard Inquiry into historic child sex abuse recently set up by the government.[5]

The church is different however in two ways. First, it is a community committed to holiness. The church receives holiness as a gift from God while also being mindful that its members remain sinners in need of transformation by the sanctifying power of God. Its commitment to welcoming those who have repented of grave wrong-doing into the fellowship of those seeking such transformation therefore goes hand in hand with a commitment to taking all necessary measures to limit the scope for further harm being done within the context of its own communities and institutions, above all to those who are most vulnerable.

Second, the church is founded on the gospel of Jesus Christ within which the ideals and practices of forgiveness and reconciliation feature strongly – if not uniquely among religions. Quite what these ideas look like in the aftermath of the abuse of ministerial power and the betrayal of trust is something that is addressed in the longer, companion document to this one from the Faith and Order Commission, *Forgiveness and Reconciliation in the Aftermath of Abuse*. It is sufficient here to say that the church's responsibility for, and response to, perpetrators does not end when, after due process, they are banned from office, imprisoned or suffer other sanctions. Quite what that responsibility means is not easy to articulate, but it is part of the task of this document to name that issue and help to open up theological and pastoral approaches which are realistic, appropriate and – basically – Christian.

The purpose of this document

This document is offered by the Faith and Order Commission as one resource alongside others, including current policies and on-going training, to help the church respond appropriately to the reality of sexual abuse – a reality for which the word 'lamentable' is entirely appropriate and still inadequate.

However, lament, while often part of the story, is never the end of a Christian narrative. While acknowledging the full truth of what we see, how can we become the church we long to be in responding to the past reality and present danger of sexual abuse: a church that lives on earth, here and now, from and for the good news that in Jesus Christ God has overcome the power of sin, evil, injustice and death itself?

The three main sections that follow aim to open up some of the theological issues that arise from commitment to becoming the kind of church we should be. We hope it can be of value to all those who read it, including in particular diocesan safeguarding officers, all clergy and others with pastoral and teaching responsibilities in the church. We also hope that it can provide useful resources for training sessions and study days that bring together people with different perspectives and experiences, some perhaps having a background in theological studies and others having expertise in safeguarding and pastoral care. That could be a PCC or Church Council, or a ministry team, or a discussion group on a training day, possibly with input from a Safeguarding Adviser. We have put some questions and a 'Bible focus' at the end of each section that could be used as discussion starters in such a context, while individuals and groups might also want to think about how they would respond to the quotations that begin each section.[6]

Section 1

We should strive to be a church where those who have been hurt by abuse find compassion, and people ready to travel patiently alongside them

---

I am still having flashbacks and nightmares about the abuse. I cannot work. I cannot make relationships. Why won't somebody in the Church listen to me?
Sally, an out-of-work social worker

I told my house-group about the abuse, and all they said was 'Just get over it'. I don't know if I can keep going to that church. They don't realize how long it all takes.
Jade, a student

Church in the experience of survivors of abuse

Surely our churches are places where people are accepted with love and compassion, especially if they have been hurt and are suffering pain? Yet one of the things that has been learned from listening to survivors of abuse is that churches do not always feel like 'safe enough' places for them. For many people who have experienced abuse, there are general issues around being in public places that would also apply elsewhere: preferring to have one's back to the wall, or to a pillar, or being near a door, for instance, and reticence about physical contact with strangers. The routine language, smells and imagery of church services, and some of the accepted practices, such as the expectation to kneel at the altar rail, may themselves trigger painful levels of emotional disturbance.[7]

That is not the end of the story, however. Church communities are known to be attractive to those who commit or have committed acts of sexual abuse. Some people have been sexually abused by those who work for the church and carry authority to represent it. Such profound abuse of a position of trust is bound to affect the abused person's capacity to experience any kind of compassion from the church. Church institutions are known to have been guilty of inaction and collusion when made aware of allegations of abuse, including abuse by church officers. If churches are to be safe enough places for survivors of abuse, they need assurance that this has changed. They need to know that clergy and other church officers are not reluctant about attending training and implementing safeguarding policy, or inclined to disbelieve survivors as fantasists or minimize their needs for healing and recovery.

These attitudes add to the burdens of false guilt, shame and sense of responsibility which many survivors already feel, reinforce the abuse they have suffered in the past and are utterly disastrous for rebuilding confidence in the church and creating the kind of trust that can allow the gospel to be shared.

Abuse, trauma and identity

People are affected by abuse in different ways. It may take many years, indeed decades, before someone who has been hurt by abuse can acknowledge to themselves and to others in full consciousness the wrong done to them.[8] Once that first step has been taken, there is then likely to be a further process taking many years before something like healing and restoration can be said to have occurred. Indeed, for some it may seem that point never really comes at all, while for many it will always feel precarious. Part of the picture here is the nature of trauma, which has been widely studied in recent years. Deep, vicious damage done to people, physical or psychological, often the two bound together as in torture as well as sexual or domestic abuse, has a very long timescale for recovery. Indeed, one of the amazing things is that recovery does, in many cases, happen: human beings have an astonishing capacity for resilience in the face of the most terrible trauma.[9] What does not happen, however, is that people just 'get over' experiences of this kind. There is a process, a costly journey, that needs to be undertaken. It takes time and, in most cases, patient companionship – a working alongside and 'with' the survivor.

There may also be a further dimension here that relates to the specific character of sexual abuse. In an influential study, Alistair McFadyen analysed what might be happening in the sexual abuse of children that renders it so profoundly harmful. His answer was that there are particularly far-reaching ways in which suffering sexual abuse damages the formation of identity for the child: that deep sense of who I am in relation to God, self and others.[10] Using more conventional psychological terms, others would describe overwhelming emotions of shame and guilt that leave those who have experienced abuse feeling that they are somehow responsible for what happened: it was because there is something fearfully bad about them that this fearfully bad thing happened to them. Indeed, the perpetrator may deliberately seek to inculcate such feelings in the victim, draining their inner resources for resistance in the present and for recovery in the future.

What does the church have to offer?

What is the good news that the church has to offer in this context? It is not that it has the ability to dispense some kind of miracle cure that can short-circuit the normal, painful, slow processes of healing. This is not to deny the power of God to do things that exceed our understanding, but Christian leaders and groups that think they can deliver people from the effects of being abused may well end up compounding them, not least by blaming the victim who fails to respond to their misguided treatment. Yet the church does have confidence that in Christ, evil is overcome, light shines in the darkness and death has been robbed of the final word. That confidence should give Christians the strength, courage and patience to be with survivors in the dark places through which they are likely to need to travel on the journey of healing. It should make them prepared to work – through listening, study and prayer – at finding the right words at the right time that can enable those who have been hurt by abuse to hear God's word of life. It should above all help them to wait, to wait on God's good time to bring God's gracious plans to fulfilment, with those whose lives have been scarred by human evil.

Possible questions for discussion in relation to your own church context:

1. How can your church become 'a church where those who have been hurt by abuse find compassion, and people ready to travel patiently alongside them'?
   - What is the national or diocesan guidance that needs to be taken into account in responding to this question?
   - Which biblical passages and key words for Christian teaching might be particularly relevant?

2. What responsibility do you have as a church community to identify and address those aspects of your common life that those who have experienced abuse may find difficult or distressing?

3. How do we speak of healing to those who have suffered trauma, when we have no 'cure' to offer or professional expertise of our own?

4. How does what happens to us affect who we are? Can you share any personal examples of experiences that have 'formed' you powerfully in either positive or negative ways? How might they make a difference to the way you hear the gospel message?

Bible focus

Read Psalm 88

- How do you 'hear' this passage from Scripture in the light of what you have read and what you have been discussing?
- Many psalms move from lament to thanksgiving (e.g. Psalm 22), but this one seems to stay with lament from start to finish. How can we make space for it in our prayer as Christians?
- How do we make space in our church community for people who may not find it easy to join what some think of as 'normal' worship as they struggle with profound pain?

Section 2

We should strive to be a church where those who commit abuse are called to face human justice, hear God's word of judgement and repent and believe the good news

---

Churches are a soft touch: they are so trusting. You just have to say I have taken Jesus into my heart, and they believe you.

Gary, a convicted sex-offender

I told the bishop about the priest who sexually abused me when I was an altar boy. The bishop offered me counselling; what I wanted him to do was something about the priest who still has altar boys.

Robert, a vicar

Abuse and repentance

The church is a 'school for sinners', not a club for the righteous. If it has no room for sinners, it can hardly be faithful to the one it claims to follow. When Jesus was criticized for going to the home of a tax collector, for example, he said, 'I have come to call not the righteous but sinners to repentance' (Luke 5.32). Yet seeking to engage those who have committed the sin of abuse asks some searching questions of church practice and teaching with regard to repentance.

Studies indicate that for those who overcome the many inhibiting forces against putting fantasy into action and who engage in the sexual abuse of children, there is likely to be a continuing draw that will not be easy to resist where external circumstances do not prevent the opportunity.[11] Treatment programmes for convicted sex offenders tend to operate with a 'multi-factorial' model that addresses the diversity of motivations and circumstances that combine when people commit such crimes (with 'sexual interest' appearing as only one of these). Such programmes recognize that unless the relevant factors for the particular individual are addressed, re-offending is likely whatever good intentions the perpetrator may declare. Even if these factors are given serious, focused attention, the likelihood only diminishes rather than disappearing. In such a context, what does repentance look like, and how would we know it is 'real'?

New life?

It is clear that when the phenomenon of widespread child abuse began to come to public attention, churches at local, national and international level were sometimes reluctant to concede that they needed to take the same stringent safeguarding measures as other institutions. Various factors were at work here. Some people just did not want to accept that clergy and other church members perpetrated sexual abuse. Alongside that in some cases was an inability to conceive that someone who adhered to the Christian faith – indeed may have been of apparently exemplary devotion – could be repeatedly drawn to activity so profoundly wrong. Mainstream Christianity has never denied human sinfulness, but it has also wanted to claim that the new life of faith in Christ sets us free from sin's power. Can people who appear to be really serious about living by faith still get drawn into such grave wrongdoing? McFadyen's study, referred to above, is helpful here. It explores the difficult terrain of how committing abuse distorts the will of the abuser – their capacity for free decision-making and action – in ways that also distort 'the core of personal identity'.[12]

At the same time, the church remains a community of witness to the resurrection of the crucified one: resurrection that means none of us needs to be forever bound by our sins, however terrible they may be, because God gives life beyond the death our sins carry with them. The good news is that in Christ our sins do not define us, for 'your life is hidden with Christ in God' (Colossians 3.3). The church needs to be a place where all find the space to begin to inhabit this new life, mindful that it sings the songs of David and reads the letters of Paul, both of whom had committed serious sins of which they later repented. It is therefore imperative that the church resists the powerful tendency in contemporary society to shun and dehumanize those who have been convicted of sexual abuse – to heap abuse, in a different but not wholly separate sense, upon their heads with the more or less explicit desire that it would overwhelm them. The church has to wrestle with hard questions about how to treat church members and church workers who have been guilty of abuse, for it cannot simply close its doors to them, and about how to speak to those who may have greatly valued their ministry and companionship in discipleship. The call to repentance is a call to turn to life and share in God's kingdom, not a summons to endless punishment inflicted by others or even oneself.

Judgement and justice

Repentance leads to life, but it begins as a response to God's word of judgement. It may seem unnecessary to underline God's judgement on abuse, but it is important to be absolutely clear about the seriousness needed here. Jesus said to his disciples, 'If any of you put a stumbling-block before one of these little ones who believe in me, it would be better for you if a great millstone were fastened around your neck and you were drowned in the depth of the sea' (Matthew 18.6). Too often in the past, Christians have let concerns about managing reputational, financial and legal risk suppress their consciousness of God's judgement on those who have done terrible harm to children and vulnerable adults. By doing so, they have exposed the institutional church to the judgement of God for its failure to deal with such manifest evil.

The psalmist imagines the whole world rejoicing because God 'is coming to judge the earth' (Psalm 96.13). God's judgement is good news because it promises the restoration of justice in human relations, without which there can be no peace. Seeking justice is not the opposite of love: it means striving for the right relationships within which human beings can flourish. The hope of Israel is for life in the land where 'Steadfast love and faithfulness will meet; righteousness and peace will kiss each other' (Psalm 85.10). The cross of Christ speaks of the depth of divine judgement and the depth of divine love, united in the act of divine salvation.

It is a vital part of our life and witness as a church that we cooperate and collaborate with the judiciary and the police in every way to ensure that all abusers are subject to human justice as this is commonly understood in our society. The tendency in some circumstances to deal with abusers solely within the framework of the church's own internal processes and practices, and to shield them from public accountability and judicial process, represents a very serious error of judgement. The ongoing discussion within the Church of England about how disclosure of abuse in the context of the confessional should be dealt with has posed some sharp questions here. While the answers remain under consideration, it is clear that the church should never separate the ministry of God's word of mercy and judgement from striving for justice in human relationships.

Possible questions for discussion in relation to your own church context:

1. How can your church become 'a church where those who commit abuse are called to face human justice, hear God's word of judgement and repent and believe the good news'?
   - What is the national or diocesan guidance that needs to be taken into account in responding to this question?
   - Which biblical passages and key words for Christian teaching might be particularly relevant?

2. What would be the likely reaction in your church community to the discovery that a regular worshipping member of the congregation was on the sex offenders register? As well as wanting to follow church policies and procedures very carefully, what difference would believing in God's good news make to your response to the situation?

3. What does true repentance look like? Is it a journey? If so, why do we sometimes seem to be able to travel the full distance, but sometimes find ourselves apparently unable to make much progress?

Bible focus

Read Luke 19.1-10

- How do you 'hear' this passage from Scripture in the light of what you have read and what you have been discussing?
- Jesus shocked and alienated those who might have been his supporters by the way he related to people regarded as notorious public sinners. What might it mean for us to follow him here?
- What is the relationship between welcome, repentance, restitution and salvation in this passage?

Section 3

We should strive to be a church where all people are welcomed into open and secure communities that make known Christ's reconciling peace

---

My friend went to a group of about sixty Christian survivors of abuse, and the leader asked how many go to church regularly. The answer was two.

Mary, diocesan counsellor

I was just about OK for the sex offender to come to our church, but did he really need to come to my house group?

Louise, housewife

Practising hospitality

One striking biblical metaphor for the church is the household of God (Ephesians 2.22), with Jesus as the cornerstone. At its best, a household evokes stability, warmth, safety, relationships with people who care about us, home. It is important to remember that this is not everyone's experience, but the church as household of God should be the place where God is, where people can find God, where they can live with God. Hospitality ought to be a hallmark of church life. The church offers God's welcome to all,[13] and it makes that welcome tangible through fostering communities that are both open and secure – open in that churches try to avoid creating 'filters' that make it easy for some sorts of people to join but keep others away, and secure in that church communities should be as safe as they can be from the risk of any kind of harm. Responding to sexual abuse shows up sharply some of the challenges in making this vision a reality.

The Church of England continues to have a strong commitment to welcoming children and young people, providing them with opportunities to hear the gospel and including them in its life.[14] It supports a wide range of activities that connect children and young people with the life of the church – not just church groups on a Sunday morning, but all manner of mid-week activities and also relations with local schools. This is a vital part of its ministry of hospitality. It also means, however, that in any church community, statistically there are likely to be present both adults and children who have been or are being abused, and adults and maybe children who have abused in the past or are presently abusing. It is possible that some people in the community will belong in both these categories. Moreover, in most cases they will be more or less invisible to others around them. The church's doors remain open to both, and the nature of most church communities is that they aim to encourage openness and friendship. Part of their witness to God's purpose 'to reconcile to himself all things, whether on earth or in heaven, by making peace through the blood of his cross' (Colossians 1.20) is to be consciously and deliberately hospitable to those who have experienced abuse, to those who have committed it and to those who have been accused of it and whose guilt or innocence is not clear. That remains a difficult, powerful and indeed perhaps unique witness in contemporary society. The church is committed to sustaining it because of the gospel message entrusted to it.

It must also be recognized, however, that sustaining it will be costly, in a number of intersecting ways. Such a witness requires taking steps to protect the vulnerable. Church communities need to accept their responsibilities for promoting good and safe practice, for following relevant policy guidance and for creating healthy relationships. Safeguarding policies help to ensure that abusers do not have the opportunities to groom children, families and adults to pave the way for abuse. Church communities cannot afford to be naïve about the levels of intelligence, determination and duplicity that can be shown by abusers in this respect. They must be vigilant for any signs that grooming may be happening, and ready to respond when officers or other members are told about or observe actual or potential abusive behaviour. Where church members are made aware of those who pose a risk to others, they need to take appropriate action to ensure that actual and potential victims are protected from them. They should never be content to collude with injustice, silence and denial. Sexual abuse is a serious crime before the law as well as a grave sin before God. When the sin is admitted, the legal process of trial and punishment must be faced, for the sake all concerned, as was stressed at the end of the previous section.

Challenges for a welcoming church

Following a criminal investigation where an abuser has been found guilty, can they after serving whatever sentence has been imposed be welcomed back into a local church community? Yes, but there will be clear conditions attached to their participation in congregational life, and constraints too on which congregation they can join. For instance, in the case of a Registered Sex Offender, these would preclude holding 'any official role or office in the church which gives him or her status or authority'.[15] A formal risk assessment would be necessary, following which decisions would be taken around various matters including which congregations the person can safely join, and which they cannot, in order not to put at risk a child or adult who may be vulnerable. The particular restrictions will vary greatly and be based upon the risk which that person is assessed to pose.

Does the imposition of such conditions for participating in the life of the church community mean that the church's welcome is somehow qualified or weakened? It is an important question to consider. In welcoming people into an open and secure community, the church has an obligation to help them work out how to belong within such a community. Where they are known to have behaved in a way that is utterly destructive of the trust on which it depends, it is appropriate that the welcome includes clear guidelines and requires promises to remain within them. While the terminology of contract is a natural one in our society in this context, the biblical category of covenant can serve to remind us that welcome into the people of God has always carried with it particular expectations and instructions, and that ignoring them or setting them aside has consequences. The purpose of those instructions is, as the New Testament teaches, to fulfil the law of love: to enable the people of God to be a community marked by love of God and love of one another. Because care for one another is one of the hallmarks of this community, the vulnerable must be protected and therefore proportionate restrictions applied in cases where the risk of serious harm to others is significantly increased. At the same time, a covenant is made by the assent and the pledges of all parties, and it takes account of the needs and abilities of each. In the light of these points, one can understand why both the Methodist Church of Great Britain and the Church of Scotland have chosen to use the language of covenant to describe the formal agreements they use to regulate participation in church life by offenders, along the same lines described in the previous paragraph.

Commitment to witnessing to God's welcome of all in Christ also requires churches to think carefully about what it really means to welcome those who have experienced abuse, as indicated in the first main section above. That may mean a readiness to create different kinds of communities and different kinds of spaces that are metaphorically if not literally adjacent to what may be thought of as the 'main' areas of worship and gathering. That might include occasional services or on-going groups that are especially sensitive to the needs of survivors. At the same time, without any dilution to the church's

Section 3

commitment to making safer spaces, it has to be recognized that there can never be a guarantee of absolute safety in any human context. The church as community and institution lives within the realities of human limitation and sinfulness.

As was noted at the outset, those who are prepared to speak to others in the church about what has happened to them are probably a minority of those in congregations who are suffering or have suffered abuse, and those who have been convicted of abuse are a minority of the abusers within them. Even when an allegation of abuse is made, it may or may not result in a clear judgement about guilt, and when it does the process may take some time, perhaps years. At the end of it, some people in the community may continue to believe in the person's innocence despite their conviction for the offence, or in their guilt despite their acquittal. An allegation may create profound polarization within the church community, or unite it against either the person making the allegation or the person accused. If the offence consists in viewing images on the internet, there may be a perception by the abuser and perhaps by their supporters that there are no 'victims' and therefore no abuse in this case, despite the clear legal and moral position to the contrary. Whatever has happened, there is the potential for the attention of local and even national media to be attracted in a way that may feel deeply threatening. A document such as this cannot offer a set of prescriptions for those facing these circumstances, but it can suggest how church communities and in particular those who lead them might keep at the forefront of their attention the question of the kind of community that the church needs to be in order to witness to the world concerning the treasure of the gospel.

The abuse of power

The reality of abuse generates some hard-edged questions, questions that are both theological and practical, as the preceding paragraphs have tried to show. While they may not come with the same sense of urgency as those reviewed so far, some of the most difficult issues here are about the kind of culture that may help create the opportunities for abuse to occur and to remain undetected. Given that abuse corrodes the kind of community that the church needs to be in order to witness to the gospel, are there features of our corporate life that may contribute to a climate where abuse can take hold?

All abuse is an abuse of power, and all abuse relies on an imbalance and related use of power.[18] Churches can be communities where such imbalance is very evident, not least in the way that different kinds of power can constellate around the clergy: the power of ritual leadership, the power of being entrusted with intimate secrets, the power of having the strongest voice both in making the community's critical decisions and in shaping its culture and attitudes. Nor do clergy always find it easy to acknowledge such power, to ensure they are accountable for the way they use it and to share it consciously with others as they exercise the particular authority they have been given to preach the gospel and administer the sacraments. Communities where power is held and deployed without awareness of the temptations it carries with it and without regard to the institutional restraints set in place for it – including, for the Church of England, Canon Law – are not open and are not secure. Those who hold office in the church at whatever level who think they are exempt from all that because of their fine intentions or unique situation tread on treacherous ground.

Part of the church's response here needs to be a theologically grounded account of how power is used well. How can power enable hospitality? How can it hold the difficult tensions that have been sketched out with regard to the church's ministry of welcome, and do so with care and creativity? There is much interest in the contemporary church in leadership,[19] and all leadership is an exercise of power. As such, while inherently containing temptations to abuse, leadership also always offers opportunities to work at aligning the dynamics of human power with the transforming purposes of God. Good leadership in the church, therefore, is a crucial element in how the church builds communities that are both open and secure, within which people can know Christ's reconciling peace.

Good neighbours

The start of this section spoke of the New Testament imagery of the church as household, *oikos* in Greek. The New Testament also, however, uses language associated with *polis*, which is often translated 'city' but overlaps with what we might term 'society' or 'the public sphere', and is indeed the root of the English term 'politics'.[20] This suggests that the church is at its best when it is both personal and public – where the local church can provide familial caring, nurture and discipline along with wider accountability to the public sphere. A recent piece of research by the Church Urban Fund and Theos elaborates this further.[21] They offer a strong argument for the value and worth of the 'neighbourliness' that local churches can offer as a means of bringing people together in a lonely and individualist society. They argue for valuing the strength and quality of local relationships and suggest that 'neighbourliness' should be defined as offering public value. It might be added that the tendency towards isolation of individual households from their neighbours contributes to a loss of 'safety' and greater exposure to risks of abuse.

Neighbourliness, as an expression of loving our neighbour as ourselves, is at the heart of a healthy local faith community and promotes caring and flourishing relationships. This means that the church will not be concerned only for its regular worshippers or those who happen to make it to the door of the church for a service. Rather, it will seek to be a community that offers the hospitality of Christ through all the various networks of relationships in which the members of that community participate, reaching out into many facets of wider society. Wherever it finds itself, it will want to speak of the good news that the possibility of healing, of justice and of restoration can never be shut down or closed off by human suffering. Wherever it finds itself, it will want to offer God's welcome to those who have been hurt by abuse and to those who want to turn away from their sins and live.

Possible questions for discussion in relation to your own church context:

1. How can your church become 'a church where all people are welcomed into open and secure communities that make known Christ's reconciling peace'?
2. What is the national or diocesan guidance that needs to be taken into account in responding to this question?
    - Which biblical passages and key words for Christian teaching might be particularly relevant?

- Are there some people who would not feel welcome if they turned up on a Sunday morning, despite your good intentions? Why might that be?

3. Survivors' experiences of turning to the church for help and support are hugely variable. Some have found love and acceptance, others rejection and condemnation, or just a refusal to think that anything might need to change in church life in order to make them welcome. What might be the key factors for a positive experience here, and what do they have to do with the teaching about the church and the love of God that we find in the Bible?

Bible focus

Read Colossians 3.5–17

- How do you 'hear' this passage from Scripture in the light of what you have read and what you have been discussing?
- What do we need to 'get rid of' (verse 8) in order to be faithful as Christ's church? How do we respond to those who want to belong to the church but do not seem able to 'get rid of' those things that are incompatible with the church's calling?
- If you had to pick out one sentence or phrase from this passage as a word for the church today as it seeks to face the evil of abuse, what might it be?

Afterword

We need to be a repenting and learning church that recognizes past and present failures and the harm they have caused, and seeks forgiveness from those we have failed and from God.

This document started by asking: what kind of church should we strive to be, in the face of the evil of abuse? At the end of it, it needs to be underlined that the churches have too often failed to live up to their calling in this situation, and that their failings are not simply in the past but remain part of present reality.

The first main section began with the statement that we should strive to be a church where those who have been abused find compassion, and people ready to travel patiently alongside them. Christians have too often met them instead with indifference, suspicion and incredulity. They have been reluctant to address their cry for care and their cry for justice. They have preferred to advise, preach and give their own counsel rather than to listen, learn and simply be alongside. They have thought that they know the journey to be travelled and the speed it should take, and have sometimes compounded suffering and harm through what was imagined to be pastoral ministry.

Afterword

The second main section began with the statement that we should strive to be a church where those who commit abuse are called to face human justice, hear God's word of judgement and repent and believe the good news. Christians, and in particular those with power and authority in the church, have too often accepted an appearance of repentance without probing the reality. They have wanted to hide from the glare of public condemnation and have therefore on occasions played a part in shielding people who have engaged in criminal behaviour from the light of justice. They have not reckoned with the depths of their own theological and spiritual traditions about the radical effects of human sinfulness.

The third main section began with the statement that we are called to be a church where all people are welcomed into open and secure communities that make known Christ's reconciling peace. Christian communities have too often been found closed and unwelcoming by those who have experienced abuse. They have made space for abusers to continue abusive behaviours, and while the churches as institutions do not bear sole responsibility here they must bear some. Inertia and disinterest have inhibited the consistently effective implementation of policies to reduce the risk of abuse even after the need for them became a matter of general agreement.

What does it mean for the church to repent, as opposed to individuals within the church? It is an important question, one addressed, along with others, in *Forgiveness and Reconciliation in the Aftermath of Abuse*, the companion document to this one from the Faith and Order Commission. Repentance, forgiveness and reconciliation are not just issues that churches have to address in terms of their ministry to others.

There is a need for repentance on the part of the churches for the harm they have done. There is a need to seek forgiveness from those whom they have harmed by their wrong action and their destructive neglect, and forgiveness also from God. There is a need to ask what it means to seek restoration and healing as churches in this context. Like other questions raised by this document, these are both profoundly theological and profoundly practical. It is for all of us to respond to them.

Resources for Further Study

of Theological Issues Raised by Safeguarding and Responding to Abuse

Going further (suitable for wide range of readers)

Sue Atkinson, *Breaking the Chains of Abuse: A Practical Guide* (Oxford: Lion, 2006)

__, *Struggling to Forgive: Moving on from Trauma* (Oxford: Monarch, 2014)

Anthony Bash, *Forgiveness: A Theology* (Eugene, Oregon: Cascade, 2015)

Paul Butler, 'Staying Safe', in *Clergy in a Complex Age: Responses to the Guidelines for the Professional Conduct of the Clergy*, edited by Jamie Harrison and Robert Innes (London: SPCK, 2016), pp. 37–43

Marina Cantacuzino, *The Forgiveness Project: Stories for a Vengeful Age* (London: Jessica Kingsley, 2015)

Stephen Cherry, *Healing Agony: Re-imagining Forgiveness* (London: Continuum, 2012)

Jane Chevous, *From Silence to Sanctuary: A Guide to Understanding, Preventing and Responding to Abuse* (London: SPCK, 2004)

Churches Together in Britain and Ireland, *Time for Action: Sexual Abuse, the Churches and a New Dawn for Survivors* (London: CTBI, 2002)

Graham Wilmer, *Conspiracy of Faith: Fighting for Justice after Child Abuse* (Cambridge: Lutterworth, 2007)

Going deeper (more specialized and/or may presume more academic knowledge)

Justine Allain-Chapman, *Resilient Pastors: The Role of Adversity in Healing and Growth* (London: SPCK, 2012)

Anthony Bash, *Forgiveness and Christian Ethics* (Cambridge: Cambridge University Press, 2007)

___, *Just Forgiveness: Exploring the Bible, Weighing the Issues* (London: SPCK, 2011)

Jeremy M. Bergen, *Ecclesial Repentance: The Churches Confront their Sinful Pasts* (London: T & T Clark, 2011)

Leslie Bilinda, 'Remembering Well: The Role of Forgiveness in Remembrance', *Anvil*, 30:2 (September 2014), pp. 1–12

Susan J. Brison, *Aftermath: Violence and the Remaking of a Self* (Princeton: Princeton University Press, 2002)

Brian Castle, *Reconciliation: The Journey of a Lifetime* (London: SPCK, 2014)

Church of Scotland Mission and Discipleship Council and The Safeguarding Committee, Forgiveness and Proportionality Working Group, *For of Such is the Kingdom of Heaven: Creating a Church Where All May Safely Live* (2009), available at http://www.churchofscotland.org.uk/__data/assets/pdf_file/0016/5083/forgiveness_proportionality_2009.pdf

L. Gregory Jones, *Embodying Forgiveness: A Theological Analysis* (Grand Rapids, Michigan: Eerdmans, 1995)

Marie Keenan, *Child Sexual Abuse and the Catholic Church: Gender, Power, and Organizational Culture* (Oxford: Oxford University Press, 2012)

Maria Mayo, *The Limits of Forgiveness: Case Studies in the Distortion of a Biblical Ideal* (Minneapolis: Fortress Press, 2015)

Alistair McFadyen, *Bound to Sin: Abuse, Holocaust and the Christian Doctrine of Sin* (Cambridge: Cambridge University Press, 2000)

Christine D. Pohl, *Making Room: Recovering Hospitality as a Christian Tradition* (Grand Rapids, Michigan: Eerdmans, 1999)

James Newton Poling, *The Abuse of Power: A Theological Problem* (Nashville: Abingdon, 1991)

Susan Shooter, *How Survivors of Abuse Relate to God: The Authentic Spirituality of the Annihilated Soul* (Farnham: Ashgate, 2012)

Steven Tracy, 'Sexual Abuse and Forgiveness', *Journal of Psychology and Theology*, 27:3 (1999), pp. 219–29

Miroslav Volf, *Exclusion and Embrace: A Theological Exploration of Identity, Otherness, and Reconciliation* (Nashville: Abingdon, 1994)

Rowan Williams and Michael Lapsley, 'The Journey towards Forgiveness: A Dialogue', *The Ecumenical Review*, 66:2 (July 2014), pp. 191–213

For an overview of safeguarding for children and vulnerable adults in the Church of England and links to related resources, including current policy documents and practice guidelines, go the web page on the Church of England website at https://www.churchofengland.org/clergy-office-holders/safeguarding-children-vulnerable-adults/national-policy-practice-guidance.aspx

Notes

1. While this is a Church of England document, colleagues from the Methodist Church have been involved in the drafting process, and much of the content could be adapted for use in Methodist contexts and indeed in other denominations. The Church of England is committed to maintaining a strong working relationship on safeguarding with the Methodist Church within the context of the Covenant between the two churches.
2. For current national safeguarding documents for the Church of England, see the page on 'National Policy and Practice Guidance' at https://www.churchofengland.org/clergy-office-holders/safeguarding-children-vulnerable-adults/national-policy-practice-guidance.aspx. Current policy documents for the Church of England include: Archbishops' Council, *Protecting all God's Children: The Policy for Safeguarding Children in the Church of England* 4th ed. (London: Church House Publishing, 2010); *Responding Well to those who Have Been Sexually Abused: Policy and Guidance for the Church of England* (London: Church House Publishing, 2011); *Promoting a Safe Church: Policy for Safeguarding Adults in the Church of England* (London: Church House Publishing, 2006).
3. See for instance the *Final Report of the Commissaries appointed by the Archbishop of Canterbury in relation to a Visitation upon the Diocese of Chichester*, May 2013, available at http://www.archbishopofcanterbury.org/data/files/resources/5055/Final-Report.pdf.
4. The report from Churches Together in Britain and Ireland, *Time for Action: Sexual Abuse, the Churches and a New Dawn for Survivors* (London: CTBI, 2002), was an important part of this process. For a recent statement highlighting the importance of learning from survivors, see the speech by Bishop Paul Butler to the Church of England General Synod in July 2013, available at https://www.churchofengland.org/clergy-office-holders/safeguarding-children-vulnerable-adults/media-statements-newsletters/speech-from-bishop-paul-butler-at-july-2013-synod.aspx.
5. For information on the Independent Inquiry into Child Sexual Abuse, often referred to as the Goddard Inquiry, see https://www.iicsa.org.uk/.
6. Original names have been changed for these quotations.
7. Responding Well, e.g. pp. 15–16; Time for Action, e.g. pp. 135–36; Promoting a Safe Church, e.g. pp. 10–12.
8. See chapter 4, 'The Problem with Memory', in Sue Atkinson, *Breaking the Chains of Abuse: A Practical Guide* (Oxford: Lion, 2006), pp. 34–42.
9. Justine Allain-Chapman, *Resilient Pastors: The Role of Adversity in Healing and Growth* (London: SPCK, 2012).
10. Alistair McFadyen, *Bound to Sin: Abuse, Holocaust and the Christian Doctrine of Sin* (Cambridge: Cambridge University Press, 2000), pp. 57–59.

Notes

11 David Finkelhor, *Child Sexual Abuse: New Theory and Research* (New York: Free Press, 1984).
12 McFadyen, *Bound to Sin*, pp. 107–30; the quotation is from p. 127.
13 Miroslav Volf, *Exclusion and Embrace: A Theological Exploration of Identity, Otherness, and Reconciliation* (Nashville: Abingdon, 1994).
14 Church of England Education Division and National Society, *Going for Growth: Transformation for Children, Young People and the Church*, GS 1769 (2010), available at https://www.churchofengland.org/education/children-young-people/going-for-growth.aspx.
15 *Protecting All God's Children*, pp. 49–53. In the case of a Registered Sex Offender, Church of England policy follows statutory guidelines under Multi-Agency Public Protection Arrangements that would place appropriate restrictions on the person's involvement in church life following a formal risk assessment and be explicit about sanctions for non-compliance.
16 *Protecting All God's Children*, p. 51.
17 The national 'Safe Spaces' project currently underway is one way in which the Church of England is seeking to engage respectfully with survivors of abuse, creating the right kind of environment for survivors to meet with church representatives on as it were level ground, and not making assumptions about what kind of welcome from the church would be appreciated by people who have suffered in some cases directly at the hands of those who claimed to be the church's representatives. See the 'Statement on "Safe Space" Proposal' at https://www.churchofengland.org/media-centre/news/2014/08/statement-on-safe-space-proposal.aspx.
18 See the current version of *Guidelines for Professional Conduct of the Clergy* at https://www.churchofengland.org/about-us/structure/general-synod/about-general-synod/convocations/guidelines-for-the-professional-conduct-of-the-clergy.aspx, including the comments by Francis Bridger in his appended 'Theological Reflection', together with the chapter by Bishop Paul Butler on 'Staying Safe' in *Clergy in a Complex Age: Responses to the Guidelines for the Professional Conduct of the Clergy*, edited by Jamie Harrison and Robert Innes (London: SPCK, 2016), pp. 37–43.
19 Church of England Faith and Order Commission, *Senior Church Leadership: A Resource for Reflection* (2015), available at https://www.churchofengland.org/about-us/work-other-churches/faith-and-order-commission.aspx.
20 Luke Bretherton, *Christianity and Contemporary Politics: The Conditions and Possibilities of Faithful Witness* (Chichester: Wiley-Blackwell, 2010), p. 150.
21 Church Urban Fund and Theos, *Good Neighbours: How Churches Help Communities Flourish* (2014), available at http://www.theosthinktank.co.uk/publications/2014/07/10/good-neighbours-how-churches-help-communities-flourish, p 57.